Paulie's Love Catering presents
Taste the Love:
Ordinary Foods with Extraordinary Flavors

by Paulette Johnson Elliott

Copyright © 2020 by Paulette Johnson Elliot

All rights reserved. This book or any portion thereof may not be reproduced or used in any manner whatsoever without the express written permission of the publisher except for the use of brief quotations in a book review.

Printed in the United States of America

First Printing, 2020

ISBN 978-0-578-80679-2

Paulie's Love
Charlotte, North Carolina

www.paulieslovescatering.com

DEDICATION

This book is dedicated to my daughter, Janeece C McDonald, and my husband, Martin R Elliott, for believing in me and the gift that God gave me when I didn't believe it fully myself. Thanks, family, for pushing me to limits so the world can taste and see.

This book is also dedicated to everyone who fought through physical illnesses and hard battles to pursue and follow their dreams, pushing past circumstances and obstacles and low self-esteem and depression. Beating the odds. Fight until there is no more fight in you to accomplish your goals and dreams. Continue to push forward. Keep believing. Understand the process and believe that faith is the substance of things hoped for and the evidence of things not seen.

ACKNOWLEDGMENTS

I would like to extend my sincerest gratitude to the following individuals:

- Mary E. Johnson
- William and Gwendolyn Johnson
- David and Denise Green
- Bishop David J. Billings
- Janeece C. McDonald
- Joseph Smith
- Agnes Jackson
- Pamela Green Pringle
- Departed William Fenner
- Kecia Edey
- Judith Jamison
- Jacqueline Thomas
- PoshStyles
- DS Kimberly Alexander
- Kola Roberts
- Bishop Archie L. McInnis, II and Cynthia McInnis
- Full Effect Churches
- Pastor Yvette Whitfield, Love Life Church
- Bishop Archie McInnis, Sr. & Mother Beverly McInnis
- New Life Pentecostal Holiness Church
- Yvonne Elliott Roberts
- Courtney and Marion Callender
- Linda Johnson
- Ricky White
- Sarah Atkinson
- Lamont and Dawn McCain
- Sandy McInnis Maxwell
- Departed Brother Anthony M Johnson.
- Departed Mother Tina Gates
- Tanya Morrison
- Diana Brown
- 50 Square Feet kitchen
- Eric and Chimeen Oden
- Andrew and Kenyetta John
- Terrance and Latisha Barcliff
- Bishop Eric R. and Lady Doreen Figueroa
- New Life Tabernacle
- Pastor Steven Furtick, Elevation Church

Thank you to everyone who believes in my gift and hired me. I am thankful for all of my customers and everyone that enjoys Paulie's Love Catering.

A special thanks to Wanza Leftwich, the person who pushed me to limits and believed that I could accomplish this book and much more. She is a courageous believer!

FOREWORD

In the early days, I fell in love with Paulette's cooking. I believe that she can make cardboard taste delicious. That is how good she is in the kitchen. One of the things that immediately comes to mind is the delicious pork that she makes. The pork is so good that I would ask her to make it all the time.

One day I was enjoying the pork so much that I did not realize that I was overeating. That is how delicious it was. I started to feel a little lightheaded. I said to my wife, Cynthia, "I do not know why I'm starting to feel lightheaded all of a sudden." She replied, "Maybe it's all that pork you're eating."

I laughed because she was right. I had never tasted pork so good before that I had overindulged in the pleasure of it. The overeating was my fault, but Paulette put her foot in that pork.

That's what they say when a person has done something exceptional. Paulette is, without a doubt, an exceptional cook. After some time, I noticed that Paulette's food was so good because she loves to cook, and she loves to see people enjoying their food. She cooks from her heart and soul.

Through her cooking, she expresses her love to friends, family, and anyone else she may encounter. Whenever you are thinking about ordering good food for a party, having anything catered, or cooking a small dinner at home for your loved ones, think Paulie's Love Catering. Her recipes are made from love and will make anyone joyful at a dinner table as they indulge the delicious spices of any meal she creates.

If you love your friends and family and want them to feel your love, you will be glad that you chose Paulie's Love Catering.

Bishop Archie L. McInnis, II

WORDS FROM CHEF ADAM DIETRICH

Noted food writer and cookbook author, James Beard, once wrote, "Food is our common bond, a universal experience." Paulie's Love exemplifies this quote through the love and passion shown in each recipe. I've had the honor of a lifetime to be with Paulette in the kitchen through her training and have experienced her love of food and hospitality.

Recipes in this book were meticulously tested, tested and chef approved! I hope that you find the same joy in making these recipes as Paulette did in creating and writing them.

To my dear friend Paulette:

I am so proud to be a part of this wonderful cookbook and to see this dream of yours come to reality. I wish you many years of success and joy in this wonderful business of feeding people.

Chef Adam Dietrich, Culinary Instructor

Phillip Van Every Culinary Arts Center at Central Piedmont Community College

A NOTE FROM PAULIE

I am so excited to present this book to the world! I have been working on this book for many years, and finally, I'm getting it to the masses. I am Paulette Elliott, owner and founder of Paulie's Love Catering, where you experience ordinary food with extraordinary flavors. This book has been inspired by my love for food, sharing it with everyone who has been a part of my life and my incredible travels. I express myself through my food, and it tells my story.

This cookbook is filled with authentic food with bold flavors. This is not just a salt and pepper cookbook. Whoever follows these recipes must have patience and love while cooking. Trust me, anyone would be proud to cook any of these fine dishes.

My culinary journey started when I was a little girl. I watched my mother cook and sat around the table with my siblings enjoying our family meals. My mother spoke through her cooking. She told her family she loved and cared for us through her food the same way I speak love through my meals. My journey with food stems from family, love, and my travels. I am blessed to have a husband like I do. Before we got married, he asked me where I wanted to travel to and why. My answer always was to learn about food. I always wanted to learn different styles of cooking and seasonings every time I have traveled.

After we married, we traveled to Las Vegas for our honeymoon, where I went to Emeril's restaurant. My husband and brother-in-law asked if the Head Chef would come to meet me. I felt like I met the president. My husband saw the fire and excitement in my eyes that night, and he's been pushing me to expand my cooking skills ever since.

We have traveled to the Dominican Republic, Puerto Rico, Mexico, and Aruba to embrace the Latin and Spanish cultures of cooking. We have also traveled to Jamaica, Saint Thomas, Cayman Islands, and the Bahamas to learn the Caribbean styles. In the United States, we traveled to Dallas, Texas, Miami, Florida, and my favorite, New Orleans, Louisiana, where the experience of the food and flavors is priceless. Next stop, Italy and France.

I have tasted some of the best foods in the world and learned so much about the art of cooking. This has impacted my life and cooking. The flavors, colors, and spices that I have experienced are in the recipes I present to you in this culinary love letter.

So, join me on this journey of food, flavors, and Paulie's Love cooking.

PAULIE'S RULES FOR COOKING

1. Wash your hands as it prevents the spreading of germs.
2. Wear gloves.
3. Display all materials needed for preparation.
4. Make sure you have all the ingredients.
5. Follow the directions.
6. Keep the area around you clean and neat.
7. Be patient and allow food to cook for the appropriate time

PAULIE'S LOVE MENU

APPETIZERS
Jerk Shrimp Deviled Eggs
Lump Crab Coleslaw
Lemon Lime Love Wings

MAIN DISHES
Yard Style Braised Stewed Oxtails
Blackies Jerk BBQ Chicken
Paulie's Love Salmon
Paulie's Style Ham
Lobster Four Cheese Mac 'N Cheese
Brooklyn Seafood Jambalaya

SIDES
Paulie's Sticky Candied Yams
Momma's Collard Greens
Coconut Rice 'N Peas

DESSERTS
Pecan Sweet Potato Pie
The Big Apple Pie
Paulie's Bread Pudding

APPETIZERS

JERK SHRIMP DEVILED EGGS

This dish was inspired by my love for culinary school. When I walked in that big kitchen with about 15 stoves grills fryers and everything you can imagine, it looked like kitchen heaven! My heart was raising with excitement. I kept saying, "I'm really doing this, and I'm in it 'til the end." I kept speaking my accomplished goals to myself. My dream, my love. I felt so comfortable. I was never late or absent. I was pumped. A lifelong dream was now my reality. It was hard work. After cooking, the kitchen had to be thoroughly cleaned, and I wasn't turned off a bit. It assured me of my gift and my love for the joy of cooking.

My instructor calls me the mother of the kitchen. His name is Chef Adam Deitrick (Chef D is what we called him!) Talk about passion for the skill. It spilled out his pours. It's like he had a radar of who was really in it and who just wasn't sure. He would give me cookbooks to study and bring back. He also gave me lessons on controlling food costs. He really saw the fire in my eyes. After passing the test and receiving My license, we had a showcase, and this appetizer was a showstopper!

YIELD
12 servings

PREP TIME
15 minutes

COOK TIME
40 minutes

INGREDIENTS
12 *eggs*
½ *cup of mayonnaise*
1 *tablespoon of Dijon mustard*
1 *teaspoon of Apple cider vinegar*
1 *tablespoon of sweet relish*
¾ *teaspoon of onion powder*
1 *pinch of salt*
1 *pinch of pepper*
Paprika, garnish as desired

JERK SHRIMP INGREDIENTS

24 large shrimp, cleaned and deveined

½ of a Scotch bonnet pepper, diced finely

1 teaspoon of thyme

1 teaspoon of onion powder

1 teaspoon of garlic powder

½ teaspoon of ginger powder

2 tablespoons of olive oil

1 tablespoon of jerk seasoning

1 tablespoon of brown sugar

1 tablespoon of soy sauce

½ a lime, juiced

2 tablespoons of parsley, chopped

¼ teaspoon of cinnamon

¼ teaspoon of nutmeg

¾ teaspoon of Allspice (pimento seed), grounded

¼ teaspoon of black pepper

DIRECTIONS

Bring water to a boil. Add 12 eggs. Allow eggs to boil for 15 minutes.

Place boiled eggs in an ice bath to stop the cooking process.

1. Once eggs have cooled completely, peel them and slice in half lengthwise. Handle with care.
2. Remove yolk to a medium bowl with a spoon. Place egg whites on a separate plate.
3. Mash the yolks with a fork and add the mayo, mustard, vinegar, relish, salt, and pepper. Stir everything until fluffy without lumps. Then cover and place in the fridge.

To cook jerk shrimp:

1. Marinate shrimp, then grill in a pan or on the grill for 2 minutes on each side.
2. As you assemble the deviled eggs, use a spoon or a piping bag to add a portion back into the egg white halves. Sprinkle with paprika and place jerk shrimp on top. You can also use bacon and or avocado! Enjoy

LUMP CRAB COLESLAW

This is a crisp and refreshing dish with a hint of sophistication. This can serve at a barbecue or as an appetizer at an elegant dinner party. The most important element of a fantastic coleslaw is how the veggies are cut. As a suggestion, use a mandolin to shred the veggies. This side dish was a blast at my husband's birthday celebration.

My greatest inspiration for making this dish from my eldest sister, Marion Y Callender. Growing up, she was the mother of the house. When my mom was at work, she would cook and clean and braid our hair and make sure we are ready for bed before mom comes, She Came to visit this spring, and I prepared fried shrimp and this coleslaw. She enjoyed it so much that she ate the whole pan! She loved it. When she kept going back for it, I knew it was a winner. This will be a blast at your social gatherings.

YIELD
12 servings

PREP TIME
20 minutes (with a mandolin)

ASSEMBLE TIME
15 minutes

INGREDIENTS

2-3 cups of lump crabmeat
½ a head of green cabbage, shredded
½ a head of red cabbage, shredded
6 carrots, peeled, cut, and shredded
½ of an onion, finely shredded or chopped
½ cup of mayonnaise
2 tablespoons of Apple cider vinegar
3 tablespoons of sweet relish
1 tablespoon of sugar
2 teaspoons of Dijon mustard
2 tablespoons of plain yogurt
¼ teaspoon of celery seeds
¼ teaspoon of salt or to taste
¼ teaspoon of pepper
1 tablespoon of parsley, chopped

DIRECTIONS

Combine all the salad ingredients, wet ingredients, and seasonings in a bowl (not the crab meat and parsley), stir, and then set aside. In another large bowl, combine green and red cabbage, onion, and carrots.

Mix together and pour the wet mixture over the cabbage mixture and incorporate all ingredients.

Place lump crab meat on top of completed coleslaw, and then sprinkle chopped parsley and paprika on top to garnish.

Place in a serving plate, chill and serve.

LEMON LIME LOVE WINGS

This chicken wing recipe was a dream!! I dreamt of this recipe and woke up and wrote it down. Jacqueline Thomas, a client of mine, was getting married, and she had family members that flew in the day before her wedding. She ordered several types of dishes, but when she added wings, I asked her if I could "jazz them up." She said, "Sure!" So, I cooked a large pan of them. To my surprise, she called me and was raving about the food, but the wings were the showstopper. She then ordered two more pans, and two years later, she is still ordering these wings. Try it!

YIELD
10 servings

PREP TIME
20 minutes*

*Note: You will need 3 bowls and 3 prep stations.

COOK TIME
35 minutes

PREPARATION NOTES
While preparing chicken, please use gloves and wash hands. Prep area before and after with a bacteria-killing soap or spray. Keep the area clean and free from germs.

CHICKEN INGREDIENTS

5-8 lbs of wings
2 teaspoons of seasoning salt
1 tablespoon of black pepper
1 tablespoon of garlic powder
1 tablespoon of onion powder
1 tablespoon of paprika
3 packs of Sa'zon seasoning
1 teaspoon of ginger powder
1 tablespoon of Dijon or yellow mustard
Marinate for 2-3 hours

LOVE SAUCE INGREDIENTS

1 tablespoon of lemon zest
1 tablespoon of lime zest
1 whole lemon, juiced (remove seeds)
1 whole lime, juiced (remove seeds)
½ a lemon, thinly sliced, garnish
½ a lime, thinly sliced, garnish
1 tablespoon of finely cut parsley, garnish
4 tablespoons of honey
2 tablespoons of crushed red pepper flakes (or desired amount)

FLOUR INGREDIENTS

3 cups of all-purpose flour
1 cup of corn starch
1 teaspoon of onion powder
1 teaspoon of garlic powder
1 teaspoon of black pepper
1 teaspoon of paprika
½ teaspoon of salt

DIRECTIONS

Stir together in a bowl and set aside.

After cleaning chicken wings with cold water and lemon juice, rinse with cold water and place chicken in a large bowl. Add seasonings listed under Chicken Ingredients. Mix and marinate then place in the fridge.

Clean the area, then get another large bowl or bag and incorporate all the ingredients under Flour Ingredients. Mix and set aside.

In a large nonstick pot or fryer, add 1 - 3 cups of vegetable oil or corn oil and heat to 340 degrees.

Place wings in the four mixture until totally covered, and then place wings in (hot) oil. Allow chicken to fry for 10 minutes or until golden brown.

After all the wings are fried well, taste one. It should be crunchy but not hard. Place in a nice serving pan, then drizzle the LOVE SAUCE over all the wings. Use the lemon and lime slices and chopped parsley as a garnish! You will be licking your fingers and lips. Enjoy!

MAIN DISHES

YARD STYLE BRAISED STEWED OXTAILS

Oxtails can be cooked in several ways. This recipe has my own spin on it. This recipe was my footprint in Charlotte, NC. My friends and staff from three major businesses patronized me greatly. They gave excellent feedback, and it spoke volumes. Customers always triple their orders once oxtails are on the menu.

My greatest inspiration comes from my husband, Martin Elliott. He loves them. I have to make two orders for him as well. He loves the tender texture as well as the robust flavors. I can't make this stuff up. 'The flavor is explosive," he says. The faces he makes when he eats my oxtails are priceless. He nods his head and says, "Babe, you've done it again!"

This recipe takes love and patience.

YIELD
6-8 people

PREP TIME
20 minutes

COOK TIME
3 ½ hours

INGREDIENTS
3-4 lbs of oxtails, cut into 1-inch pieces

2 tablespoons of seasoned salt

1 tablespoon of garlic powder

1 tablespoon of onion powder

1 tablespoon of black pepper

1 teaspoon of paprika

2 tablespoons of browning (burnt sugar)

In a separate bowl combine:

1 teaspoon of Worcestershire sauce

1 tablespoon of sugar

2 tablespoons of ketchup

1 tablespoon of pimiento seeds (7-8 seeds)

1 scotch bonnet pepper, deseeded and chopped*

*Note: Wear gloves, please.

1 tablespoon of thyme

2 tablespoons of grated ginger (or 1 tablespoon of powdered ginger)

1 red pepper, cut

1 green pepper, cut

1 large onion, cut

1 tomato, cut

4 cloves of garlic, finely chopped

4 stalks of scallions, cut

2 carrots, cut

1 cup of butter beans

DIRECTIONS

Clean and trim fat off oxtails, clean with cold water and vinegar, rinse, and place in a large bowl. Add seasoned salt, black pepper, onion powder, garlic powder, and browning. Place in the refrigerator for 3 to 6 hours or overnight to marinate.

Pour two tablespoons of oil in a large pot. Place on medium heat until pot is hot. Place marinated oxtails into the hot pot and allow them to brown on both sides. All sides should brown.

Add 3 cups of water and 1 cup of beef stock into the pot. Allow oxtails to boil for 2 hours. As the water cooks down, add 1 cup of water at a time. Cook until fork punctures the meat easily. Then, add all other fresh vegetables and ingredients in the separate bowl into the pot. Stir and slow cook for 1 hour or until oxtails are tender and the gravy is thick and flavorful. Serve with rice and peas.

BLACKIES JERK BBQ CHICKEN

Getting off the plane watching the ladies dance with their big wide petticoat dresses from the 1940s. Just beautiful, Air Jamaica, made you feel like you've just landed in Paradise, that's all I wanted was music and Jerk chicken. The taste of it. The flavors made you keep coming back. I said to myself, "I have to learn to cook this before I leave."

This recipe is the best Jamaican Jerk Chicken, which includes oven and grilling instructions! It's incredibly flavorful thanks to hours of marinating in a vibrant and deliciously seasoned marinade that can be prepared days ahead. And who can resist that dark char and wonderful spices singing in the air. This is one of the best marinade recipes you'll ever try!

I have added my own reggae vibe to it. You can just hear Dennis Brown and Gregory Issac's vocals in the air. It's brimming with fresh flavors and it may seem like a strange combination of ingredients but together they create incredible, well-balanced flavor. It all compliments the chicken perfectly. With the perfect balance of heat, sweet, and savory, this dish can cook all year round, barbecues to Christmas Eve!

This dish was inspired by my late stepfather, Emanuel Knight, who was born in Kingston, Jamaica, Jonestown. My stepfather played a major part in my love for cooking Jamaican meals. As a child, I would watch him steam fish and season meat. Every seasoning was so important. Even how he cut the vegetables or smashed the scallion instead of cutting it enhanced the flavors. I was so excited. I watched and asked questions. I would not leave the kitchen until the meal was complete. He used to say, "Blackie (my nickname), stop asking so many questions." Then he would describe it. He said, "Keep watching, and you gonna master the Jamaican style of cooking." I did! He knew I had a great love for cooking Jamaican food. Big up, Manny!

YIELD
8-10 servings

PREP TIME
20 minutes

COOK TIME
Oven: 1 hour

Grill: 45 minutes

PREPARATION NOTES
Clean the chicken with cold water and lemon juice. Do not keep chicken in a warm area. Chicken must be kept refrigerated after margination. Wash hands and use disinfected soap to clean prep area and chopping board before and after prepping chicken.

INGREDIENTS

5 lbs of chicken (leg quarters)
1 onion, minced
3 stalks of scallions, minced
2 scotch bonnet peppers, minced
3-5 cloves of garlic, minced
2 tablespoons of Allspice
3 tablespoons of dried thyme
1 tablespoon of black pepper
2 teaspoons of cinnamon
1 teaspoon of nutmeg
1 tablespoon of seasoned salt (Lawry's)
3-4 tablespoons of browning
3 tablespoons of ginger powder
2 tablespoons of jerk seasoning
½ cup of non-alcoholic beer

DIRECTIONS

Place all vegetables in the processor and blend until it becomes a paste. Pour jerk marinade into a bowl. After chicken is cleaned, place it in a large bowl. Pour jerk paste over chicken and rub seasonings over all of the pieces of chicken. All seasonings should be on chicken quarter legs.

If using the oven, preheat oven to 350 degrees Fahrenheit. If using the grill, allow the grill to heat evenly to 350 degrees Fahrenheit.

Put non-alcoholic beer in a spray bottle.

Place chicken in the oven and spray every 15 minutes. Let the chicken cook for 30 minutes on each side until chicken is well done.

Place chicken on the grill so that it is not over direct heat. Allow the chicken to fully cook with grill marks shown on each side, totaling 45 minutes or until chicken is well done. Don't forget to spray with the beer every 15 minutes. For added flavors, mix BBQ sauce with remaining jerk paste and brush over the cooked chicken.

Chop and enjoy it!

PAULIE'S LOVE SALMON

This popular recipe is very dear to my soul. It's my spin on a Jamaican dish called escovitch fish. This recipe can be used with many types of fish.

I call it Paulie's Love because it's cooked from my heart. This dish is loved by many of my new friends and my sisterhood group that Dawn Billings McCain invited me into. My inspiration comes from my mother, Mary E Johnson. She loves this dish, and she loves watching me prepare it as well.

My mother is 80 years old and has seven children: William, Anthony (departed), Yvonne, Denise, Linda, Cynthia, and then me. I'm the youngest sibling. We all have had our personal highs and lows in life, but we always have had a personal love for each other, and food has always bought us together. God has granted us all wonderful gifts. I'm grateful for mine -- cooking! Serving and bring joy through food.

YIELD
1 filleted slab of salmon

7 to 8 6-oz servings

PREP TIME
20 minutes

COOK TIME
45 minutes

INGREDIENTS

1 large onion, sliced

1 red pepper, sliced

1 green pepper, sliced

1 yellow pepper, sliced

1 orange pepper, sliced

1 Habanero hot pepper, deseeded*
*Note: Use gloves while cutting this pepper. If you want it spicy, add some seeds.

1 teaspoon of Allspice

1 teaspoon of ginger

1 tablespoon of thyme

1 tablespoon of Old Bay seasoning

1 tablespoon of garlic powder

2 ounces of vinegar

6 pimento seeds

3 tablespoons of sugar or agave

DIRECTIONS

In a separate bowl, mix the cut onions and peppers with the Old Bay, ginger, pimento seeds, thyme, garlic powder, vinegar, and sugar (or agave).

Place salmon fillets in a pan. Season lightly with Old Bay, black pepper, and garlic powder.

If using the stovetop, heat a nonstick pan on medium and add 2 tablespoons of olive oil. Once the pan is heated, place salmon in the pan and cook for 5 to 7 minutes on each side. Remove and set aside.

If using the oven, preheat oven to 350 degrees Fahrenheit. Once the oven is heated, add 2 tablespoons of olive oil in a nonstick pan and place in the oven for 15 minutes or until it is well done. Set aside.

In a separate pot, place on stove on medium heat. Add 3-4 tablespoons of olive oil. Once the oil is hot, pour in all remaining ingredients. It will sound like it's frying. Stir for 5 to 7 minutes and add 2 ounces of water and simmer for an additional 3 minutes. Vegetables should still have a slight crunch. Pour vegetables and sauce over salmon and serve. Enjoy!

PAULIE'S STYLE HAM

This recipe is sweet, salty, and packed with flavors!

My brother-in-law, Bishop Archie McInnis, always pushed me and encouraged me to go further in my catering career. One night as he preached, he said, "Use your gift for when it don't rain." In the middle of his sermon, he said, "Paulette, you should bottle that glaze and advertise it." I knew it was God! The power behind the words can't be explained. He was speaking from his heart, and I felt it and ran with it. Since then, I have now sold over 300 jars of my ham glaze. I started promoting my business, and I've catered over 400 events, which include weddings, birthdays, family reunions, funeral repasses, and business luncheons.

My brother-in-law, David Green, inspire this dish. On Easter Sunday, in 1995, he invited me to dinner. He asked, "Can you bake a ham?" I said, "Yes," with joy. After that, every Easter morning before church, he would call me and ask, "Did you make ham?" It started with only Easter, but then he requested it for every holiday. I embraced it.

David can cook! He knows about mastering flavors, and he takes pride in the dishes he cooks. He will take over in the kitchen, and my sister will have to step aside with pride because Dave is working the pots. He is also a grill master. He cooks steaks, ribs, and chicken, among other meals with pride, knowing they will taste great.

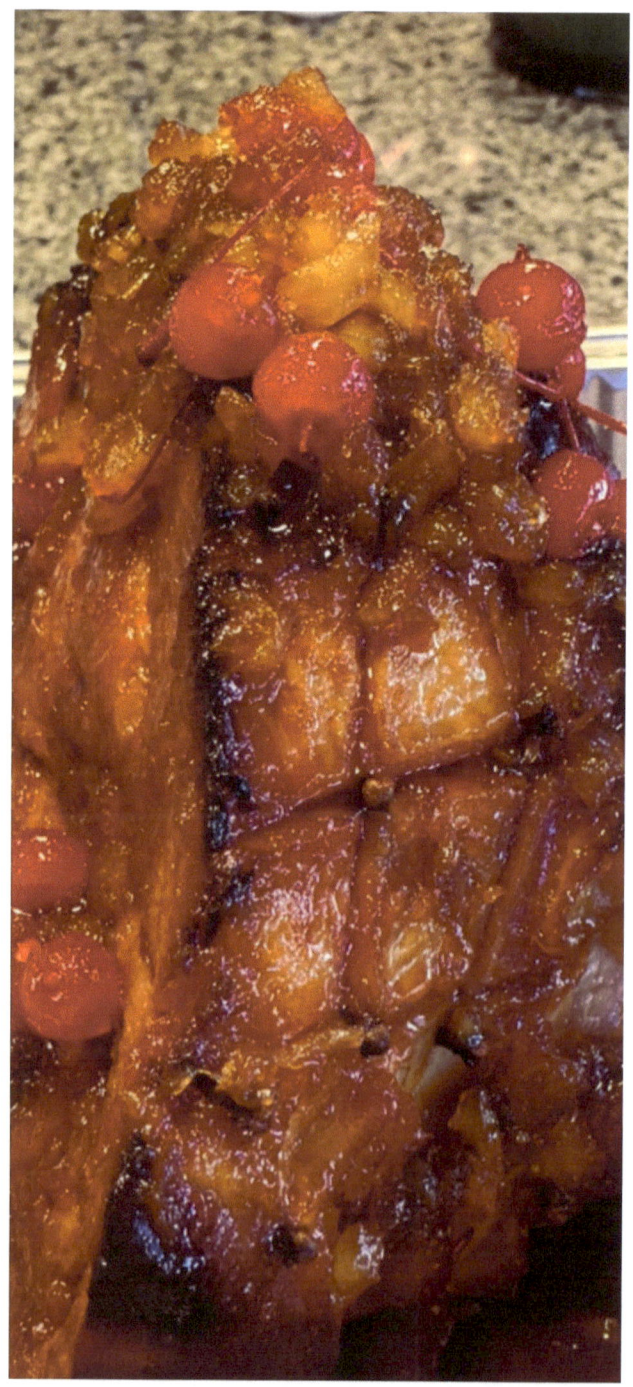

YIELD
15-20 people

PREP TIME
15 minutes

COOK TIME
2 hours 15 minutes

INGREDIENTS
4-5 lbs of smoked, cooked ham
1 can of ginger ale
15 cloves
2 jars of Paulie's Ham Glaze
1 jar of maraschino cherries
1 can of pineapple slices

DIRECTIONS
Clean the ham, then, with a sharp knife, slice horizontal lines around the top of the ham, only going ½-inch deep. After, slice vertically the same way. When it's raw, you won't see the beauty in it, but as it bakes, it will look amazing.

Place cloves all across the top of the ham, then place the ham in a deep baking pan and pour can of ginger ale over ham. Cover tightly with heavy-duty aluminum foil.

Bake ham at 350 degrees for 2 hours.

After the ham is cooked, pour off the juice from the ham and lay pineapple slices on the ham and place the cherry in the middle. Use the toothpicks to keep it from falling off. Then pour Paulie's Love Ham Glaze over the top and then place it in the oven for 15 minutes. Cut and enjoy!

LOBSTER FOUR CHEESE MAC 'N CHEESE

This is great comfort food. It doesn't matter what color you or nationality you are, Sunday dinner is not complete unless Mac 'n Cheese is on the table. Everyone loves Mac 'n Cheese! My version of Mac 'n Cheese does not go too far out of the box, but it hits those notes of comfort and flavors.

This meal was inspired by my brother-in-law, Bishop Archie McInnis. He enjoyed my cooking. He would hire me to cater his birthday celebrations at church, and my Mac 'n Cheese was always on the menu.

YIELD
15 people

PREP TIME
20 min

COOK TIME
45 min

INGREDIENTS

1 lb box of elbow noodles

1 stick of butter

1 teaspoon of season salt

1 teaspoon of black pepper

1 teaspoon of onion powder

1 teaspoon of paprika

1 teaspoon of sugar

2 eggs

1 ½ cups of whole milk

2 tablespoons of cream cheese

2 cups of Colby Jack cheese, grated

2 cups of extra sharp cheddar, grated

2 cups of mild cheddar, grated

2 cups of Monterey Jack (or sharp cheddar), grated

PAULIE'S LOVE BONUS

1 teaspoon of Old Bay seasoning

1 teaspoon of garlic powder

1 lb of large cleaned and deveined shrimp

2 large lobster tails cut

DIRECTIONS

Place a large pot of water and salt on the stove under medium heat. Bring the pot to boil and add elbow noodles. Allow to cook for 5 minutes or until noodles are done and tender. Drain and transfer noodles to a deep baking pan. Add butter and stir.

In a separate large bowl, combine milk and eggs and whisk together until thoroughly combined. Add Colby Jack, Monterey Jack, and the extra sharp cheddar cheeses along with all the seasonings and the cream cheese. Combine and stir.

Pour cheese mixture over the macaroni and stir to combine completely.

Top with the remaining mild cheddar cheese with a sprinkle of paprika over the top. Bake in a 350-degree oven for 45 minutes or until the top is golden brown, and the corners look crispy. Enjoy!

BROOKLYN SEAFOOD JAMBALAYA

This popular dish is filled with West African, French, and Spanish influences.

Growing up in East Flatbush Brooklyn, these influences were all around me, my neighbors, classmates, and close friends.

After putting my own spin and style on it, Brooklyn Jambalaya was the name for this dish. However, as I got older and studied food, New Orleans became my favorite place because of their love and creative style of cooking. France, Spain, and Africa are places where food has bold flavors. My first time visiting New Orleans, I witnessed the love, jazz music, and the joy while people at great food filled with bold and beautiful flavors. It was just amazing.

For my 9th anniversary, my husband surprised me with a trip back to New Orleans. I was excited to revisit and share the adventure with him. It was ten times better than my first visit. It is a wonderful place of love, joy, live music, and great food. Every restaurant we went to, my husband asked to meet the owner and told them I was a chef. The owner took me to see the kitchen! It was amazing! I learned how to cook Cajun food by blending, mastering, and building flavors.

This dish is about building flavors by sautéing the aromatic trinity of seasonings, onion, celery, and peppers along with andouille sausage chicken and shrimp. This dish was inspired by Martin R. Elliott because of the look on his face and the rolling of his eyes when he eat this dish. It is a look of pure satisfaction.

There are many steps to making this dish. Please follow the steps.

YIELD	PREP TIME	COOK TIME
8-10 servings	30 minutes	40 minutes - 1 hour

INGREDIENTS

1 lb of andouille sausage (or chorizo), sliced

2 lbs of chicken breast, sliced

4 lbs of large shrimp, cleaned and deveined*
*Note: Please remove the tails.

2 cups of diced onions

1 cup (2 stalks) of diced celery

1 red bell pepper, diced

1 green bell pepper, diced

4 - 5 cloves garlic, minced

3 bay leaves

1 teaspoon of thyme

1 teaspoon of oregano

2 cans of diced tomatoes

2 cans of diced chilies

3 cups of chicken broth

2 tablespoons of Slap ya Momma creole seasoning

1 teaspoon of crushed red pepper flakes

½ teaspoon of hot sauce

¼ teaspoon of cayenne pepper

2 teaspoons of Worcestershire sauce

1 cup of cut okra (optional)

1 tablespoon of sugar

3 cups of parboiled rice (Uncle Ben's preferred)

3 teaspoons of parsley, garnish

Bonus: 1 lb of king crab legs, chopped in 2-inch pieces

DIRECTIONS

Step 1: Place 2 teaspoons of oil in a pan. Heat the pan on medium heat. Cook sliced sausage for 5 minutes until browned. Remove sausage and place in a bowl.

Step 2: In the same pan, cook sliced chicken breast until well done and remove from pan. Put the chicken in the bowl. Deglaze the pan. Keep the oil from the sausage and chicken breast.

Step 3: Heat the large pot. Add the oil and the deglazing liquid and bits. Add 2 teaspoons of oil to the heated pot.

Step 4: Sauté onions, bell peppers, and celery for 1 minute. Stir in tomatoes and chilies. Add creole seasonings, thyme, oregano, red pepper flakes, bay leaves, and sugar. Add Worcestershire sauce, chicken, and sausage and stir. Cook 5 minutes while stirring occasionally. All seasoning should be in the pot except for the parsley. Optional, add okra.

Step 5: Add the rice and then add the chicken broth. Bring to a boil. Add crab legs (optional). Reduce heat to low-medium for 20-25 minutes or until liquid is absorbed and rice is cooked while stirring occasionally.

Step 6: Place large shrimp on top of the jambalaya mixture. Stir thoroughly gently and cover with a lid. Allow to simmer for 5-6 minutes until shrimp is thoroughly cooked (pink). Garnish with parsley and serve.

SIDES

PAULIE'S STICKY CANDIED YAMS

This dish is very popular in my family's house for the holidays. This dish was inspired by my late brother, Anthony M Johnson. He would take me to exquisite restaurants and order grilled octopus, clams and squid ink pasta, and sushi. He would say that he wanted me to train my pallet.

He was a captain of corrections in New York City. He was into health and wellness, but he would enjoy a good fatty dish. He didn't eat pork or red meat, so side dishes were his thing. Every time he would eat my food, he would start a 30-minute lecture about me needing to open my restaurant. He would go on and on about how much the world needs my great food.

I miss him mainly because he drilled this in my head: "Whatever you cook, put your all into it. Imagine this meal is up before the judges. Don't half step and never substitute." I miss him dearly. When my catering business started getting busy, I went and placed my business card on his burial stone to say, "I'm busy now, and you're not here to help me."

Paulie's Sticky Candied Yams is a delicious side dish that combines sweet yams, with butter, sugar, and spices. They are rich, tender, and full of flavor. I can promise they will be popular with everyone at the table. It doesn't have to be a holiday to enjoy this great side dish. These candied yams are so buttery and sweet that they practically melt in your mouth.

YIELD
8-10 people

PREP TIME
20 minutes

COOK TIME
45 minutes

INGREDIENTS

5-8 large Garnet yams, peeled and sliced oblong thin

2 sticks of salted butter, chopped in small squares

2 tablespoons of pure Vanilla extract

1 cup of white sugar

2 cups of brown sugar

¼ teaspoon of salt

1 tablespoon of cinnamon

½ teaspoon of nutmeg

½ teaspoon of Allspice

½ teaspoon of ginger

DIRECTIONS

After the yams are washed and cut into oblong ½-inch pieces, place the yams in a large deep baking pan. Preheat oven to 350 degrees Fahrenheit. Add cinnamon, nutmeg, Allspice, salt, and ginger to yams and stir with hands. Make sure seasonings are on all pieces of the yams.

Add vanilla extract followed by the white sugar and brown sugar. Add cold butter pieces, spread pieces over the top of the yams. Add 2 tablespoons of water to the corner of the pan and cover tightly with heavy-duty aluminum foil.

Once the oven is heated, place a large pan of yams in the oven and cook for 45 minutes. You should smell the aroma around after 45 minutes has passed. Remove foil and cook for 10 minutes uncovered or until sauce becomes thickened and it looks sticky. Enjoy!

MOMMA'S COLLARD GREENS

Collard greens is truly food for the soul. Country style greens is a must-have at any holiday table. I'm talking greens so good that the juices is a delicacy to drink. Pot liquor is the name. Growing up, my mom would cook collard greens and cornbread, so good that you just couldn't have one without the other. My aunt, Sarah Atkinson, was also an amazing cook. Her collard greens would melt in your mouth, I called her on the eve of Thanksgiving to ask her the same questions, and she looked forward to my call. She would pour white cornbread mix over her greens, and it cooked over the greens, incorporating the juices. Dumplings were always served with her greens. Talking about southern cooking in Brooklyn!

My greatest inspiration for this dish comes from mother, Beverly McInnis, First Lady of the New Life Pentecostal Church. She is a true rider for Christ. She stands on the righteousness of God, and she takes her spiritual life very seriously. She also never held back on encouraging others to live for Christ. She told me that God has given me a great gift of cooking. The power of God in her deep voice ran through my body, and tears began to run down my face. She loves to and believes in sowing into the gift that God gave me.

She hired me for the Holy Mount Zion Reunion. I was so excited. I was so honored and humbled that I didn't know what to charge. Because of her, I was also asked to cater the Lide/McInnis Reunion, which consisted of over 250 people. Collard greens were always on the list. Mother loved my greens so much that she gave me a set of pots, and one of them is for collard greens! To this day, I use that pot, mainly as a symbol of my love for her and her love for my cooking.

Collard greens is a dish where the hard work starts with picking out the collards. If the leaf is too large, the greens are tough, or too yellow or have black marks, don't use them. Soak and clean three times. Collards have a lot of dirt and grit, so use a little salt and cold water. Clean the leaves, stack them, and cut out the stem. Start with the largest one and move to the smallest. After, roll them until it looks like a log. Then slice them ½ inch. Greens should look like ribbons. You can slice thin or thick. Your preference.

YIELD
10-15 people

PREP TIME
20 minutes

COOK TIME
3-4 hours

INGREDIENTS

5 lbs of collard greens, cleaned and sliced
4 smoked turkey legs
Or
4 ham hocks
2 tablespoons of vinegar
2 tablespoons of brown sugar
3 tablespoons of oil
1 onion, chopped
3-4 cloves of garlic. minced
1 teaspoon of thyme
1 tablespoon of crushed red pepper flakes
1 tablespoon of black pepper
3 cups of chicken stock
2 cups of water

DIRECTIONS

Place a large pot of water on high heat and place smoke meat into boiling water. Allow meat to boil until cooked. The meat will start to break up. The water should be low. Add the chicken stock and all seasonings listed and stir. Add collard greens and turn the heat on medium. Allow greens to cook for an additional 1-2 hours until well done. Do not overcook them. Check on greens every 15 minutes. Stir until meat is incorporated into greens. Enjoy!

 # COCONUT RICE 'N PEAS

This is the authentic Jamaican rice and peas dish with my style. Jamaicans call it rice and peas, but actually, what's used is red kidney beans, not peas.

I have a fabulous way of cooking this, and this recipe hasn't failed me yet. My sister, Cynthia McInnis, would brag to all of her friends how her sister makes the best rice and peas. Every year Full Effect Gospel Ministries would have a woman's conference. I was honored to cook lunch, and my rice and peas would be the star dish on the menu.

My greatest inspiration for this dish comes from my only biological daughter, Janeece C. McDonald. She loves my cooking, and she never turns down rice and peas. When she was a child, I would make rice and peas on Sundays. She would watch me grate the coconut, and if there were ever leftovers, she would eat that instead of breakfast. Now my daughter is 25 years old and an exceptional cook.

It's really not hard to cook. You just have to follow the recipe. Green pigeon peas are also commonly used, and they taste amazing.

Coconut is the main ingredient that's incorporated in the water while the peas are cooking. Coconut milk in the can is one way it can be done, but the best way to make it is when you crack the coconut, scoop out the white meat (copra) and then purée it in the blender with water until it looks like milk. Strain 3 times (you don't want any pieces of coconut in the rice), and then set aside until the peas are half cooked, then add.

YIELD
15 people

PREP TIME
20 minutes.

COOK TIME
2 hours

INGREDIENTS

1 lb of red kidney beans, dried

½ teaspoon of ginger powder

4 cloves of garlic, minced

1 tablespoon of black pepper

1 tablespoon of thyme, dried

8-9 pimento seeds (or 1 teaspoon of ground Allspice)

1 whole scotch bonnet pepper (habanero)*

*Note: Do not remove the stem.

4 stalks of scallions, cleaned

2 tablespoons of salt

1 tablespoon of sugar

1 ½ cups of fresh coconut milk (or 1 can of unsweetened coconut milk)

3 cups of water

2 ½ cups of parboiled rice

3 tablespoons of butter

DIRECTIONS

Place cleaned beans in a large, sturdy nonstick pot with 3-4 cups of water and 2 tablespoons of salt. Allow peas to boil on high heat until water is reduced and peas are half cooked. Add garlic, black pepper, scallions, scotch bonnet pepper, coconut milk, thyme, pimento, ginger, and sugar. Cover pot. Bring to boil (45 minutes) until peas are tender. Add rice and butter (add little water if it's not covering the rice), stir and put heat on low and let rice cook slow (20 minutes).

Remove scotch bonnet pepper and discard. Remove scallions and pimento seeds as well. Take a fork and fluff up the rice. Allow the pot to simmer for 10 minutes. Serve

DESSERTS

PECAN SWEET POTATO PIE

This idea came from my love for sweet potato pie and pecans. This homemade pie is sweetened with dark brown and white sugar and flavored with these beautiful autumn warm spices. The pie filling is made solely with butter. However, the crust is made with butter and a little vegetable shortening to enhance the flakiness. It's okay to buy a pie crust. Selling these pies was so easy. My buddy, Cassandra Smith, would be first to put her order in. She just loves it. This recipe will be number one on your Thanksgiving table.

This recipe inspiration comes from a place that brings wonderful memories and joy to my heart. At age 17 years old, I witnessed the beauty and newness of Sunday morning service and ladies with pretty outfits and hats to match. I remember praise and worship, shouting and praise dancing, and singing in the choir. I was in the alto section, catching the Holy Spirit.

At this time, Pastor (now Bishop) Eric Figueroa was not only the Pastor, but he was also the choir director, the musician, the preacher, and whatever else was needed. His wife, Lady Doreen Figueroa, would sing so amazingly that you would think the heavens opened up. The church was powerful. When it was over, and they said, "Amen," we all rushed downstairs to this round table filled with sweet potato pies. If you took your time after service, you would miss out. The pies were so good that people went from slices to ordering the whole pies. That's how tasty they were.

Mother Minnie Figueroa sold pies as her fundraiser. Mother Minnie was a beautiful, graceful woman with style and a polite personality. She was tall and slim. Her voice was deep but soft, and she dressed exquisitely (Joan Crawford style). Mink coats, 6-inch heels, and beautiful hats to match her outfits. She was the true epitome of glamour. She would bake the best sweet potato pies, sweet and buttery, and the Crust was flaky (Not store-bought crust). The crowd around the table, oh my!

Mother Minnie never shared her secret, so my first time baking pies, I just kept a visual of Mother Minnie's beautiful smile and her passion as she served her sweet potato pies. The bragging rights were all over her face. Mother Minnie's pies.

HOMEMADE PIE CRUST RECIPE

YIELD
2 pie crusts

PREP TIME
15 minutes

COOK TIME
1-2 hours

INGREDIENTS
2 ½ cups of All-Purpose flour

1 ¼ teaspoon of salt

6 tablespoons of unsalted butter, chilled and cubed

¾ cup of vegetable shortening

½ cup of iced water

¼ teaspoon of cinnamon (optional)

DIRECTIONS
Using a large bowl, mix flour and salt together. Add cold butter and shortening using a pastry cutter or 2 large forks or hands with gloves.

Cut the butter and shortening into the mixture until it looks like coarse meal, pea-size bits mixed into the flour. The pastry cutter makes this process faster and easy.

Measure ½ cup of iced water in a cup and drizzle in the cold water one tablespoon at a time and cut or stir in the flour mixture with a rubber spatula after every spoon added. Do not add extra water; the dough will begin to form large clumps. Add flour to a hard, cleaned surface, pour the dough out on the surface, and with floured hands form a ball. The dough should not be sticky. Divide the ball in two equal parts. Flatten into ½-inch thick disks using your hands.

If you are not ready for it, wrap each dough ball in plastic wrap and then refrigerate for at least 2 hours before use. Roll out chilled pie dough and be gentle when placing the dough in the pie dish. This pie crust can be used for any pie.

PECAN SWEET POTATO PIE FILLING

YIELD
2-3 pies

PREP TIME
1 hour

BAKING TIME
1-2 hours

INGREDIENTS

6 to 8 large sweet potato (orange)
½ cup of chopped pecans
½ cup of heavy cream
2 sticks of unsalted butter
½ cup of dark brown sugar
½ cup of white sugar
1 tablespoon of corn starch
2 large eggs
1 tablespoon of pure Vanilla extract
1 teaspoon of cinnamon
½ teaspoon of nutmeg
¼ teaspoon of Allspice
¼ teaspoon of ground ginger
Pinch of salt

DIRECTIONS

Place large sweet potatoes in a large pot, boil for one hour, or until potatoes are soft. Cool, peel and place in a large bowl

Or: Wash potatoes and place on a large flat pan, stick with fork and allow potatoes to bake at 350 degrees Fahrenheit for 1 hour or until fork-tender. I prefer this method because baking keeps more of the yam flavor. Peel and place potatoes in a large bowl.

Using a handheld mixer, beat the potatoes on medium-high until potatoes are smooth. Combine all ingredients except the pecans.

Once everything is mixed together and there are no lumps, take a rubber spatula and push the sides and incorporate the bits on the sides. Taste and see if it needs any more ingredients and mix well.

Take pie crust dish and poke holes in the bottom of the crust. Pre-bake crust for 10 min, add pie filling evenly, and then bake for 45 minutes at 350 degrees Fahrenheit. Add pecans and bake 15 additional minutes or until well done.

Remove from oven and allow pie to cool for 20 minutes to an hour.

Note: If you notice your crust is getting dark too soon, take the foil and wrap it around the edges of the crust until pie is done. The foil will stop the crust from over-browning.

THE BIG APPLE PIE

The Big Apple Pie. I was born and raised in Brooklyn, NY, and this pie's flavor represents my city. The Big Apple! This is the best homemade apple pie you'll ever make, not only because of the flaky crust but also the spiced apple pie filling. I used a combination of apples to bring out the best flavors. I filled butter between the layers and baked it until the top was golden brown. There's a simple joy in preparing this pie as there is in eating it. Each bite will make your family and friends feel as if they are wrapped in a culinary hug.

Granny smith, red delicious, and honey crisp are the apples used for this recipe. While baking this pie, although this pie is loved and talked about by many, my true inspiration behind this recipe is from my sister, Linda Johnson. My sister loves apple pie. From our childhood, when she came from the store, she always would have that pie with that green wrapper. Y'all know those square pies tasted like sugar and overcooked apple jelly. Yes! I went there.

She would order apple pies every time I baked them. She would ask for pictures of my baked pies as if she can taste it through the picture. Once, she ordered food and apple pie and paid me to drive from Pennsylvania to Brooklyn. When she tasted the pie, her eyes would open wide with satisfaction, and her leg would shake with excitement and pleasure. She talked about this pie for weeks. Now she always hints on ways I can bake and ship pies to her home.

Use the same crust ingredients in the previous recipe.

YIELD
8-10 servings for a 9-inch pie

PREP TIME
30 minutes

COOK TIME
1 hour

COOL TIME
30 minutes

INGREDIENTS

3 Granny Smith apples*
3 Red Delicious apples*
3 Honey Crisp apples*
*Note: All apples are to be washed, peeled, cored, and sliced thin ½ inch
4 tablespoons of butter, chopped and cold
½ teaspoon of lemon zest
2 tablespoons of lemon juice
2 teaspoons of cinnamon
¼ teaspoon of nutmeg
¼ of Allspice seasoning
1 teaspoon of pure Vanilla extract
½ cup of white sugar
½ cup of dark brown sugar
1 tablespoon of corn starch

DIRECTIONS

Using a large bowl, place all the dry ingredients into the bowl and stir. Once all dry ingredients are combined, add the apples and stir. Add the lemon juice and the lemon zest and the Vanilla extract. Stir in all the ingredients. It will start to make its own juice. Yummy!

As you fill the crust with the apple mixture, add butter pieces into the layer of apples. Pile it up. After rolling out the second pie dough, place pie dough on top of the apple pie. Seal it by wrapping excess top crust under the bottom crust edge. Pressing edges together to seal, use a finger to make edges look like waves. Be creative. On the top of the crust, cut slits into it, or you can cut shapes. The pie needs a place for the moisture to release from pie, so the slits on top of the pie is a must.

Bake the pie for 45 minutes to 1 hour or until apples are tender and crust is golden brown. Place pie on a cookie sheet to catch drippings. Also, cover crust edges with foil for 20 minutes into baking to prevent excessive browning. Allow pie to cool for 30 minutes to an hour. The filling will thicken as it cools. Enjoy!

 # PAULIE'S BREAD PUDDING

This bread pudding recipe is very special to me. Its spices make it nourishing, rich and known as the comfort food of desserts with bold, fruity flavors. Bread pudding historians trace this desert back to the 12th century, as cooks then looked for economical, frugal ways to salvage and save money using leftover bread instead of letting it go to waste.

In the 13th century in England, bread pudding was known as a poor man's dish. But as this desert surfaced in the South, the Southerners began to add their own style to enhance this dish. In my travels, I've found New Orleans style was most satisfying. Paulie's love had to take it up another notch.

When I was a child, my family and I loved it when my mom cooked this desert. My mom would use all the leftover bread. If joy was a smell, that's exactly what the house smelled like.

This nurturing dish was inspired by my sister, Denise Green. Denise was a loving and caring person, but her strong personality made people see her differently. She was very protective of her siblings. She would fight anyone, and she would win. We still laugh about some boys she beat up as a teen. She never trusted strangers, and she was always on guard. As a young teen, she would watch everything, making sure the family was safe. She locked the windows and doors and made sure the gas was off.

I now know that was God in her. Her spiritual senses were very high. The Bible says watch as well as pray. God gave her the spirit to protect and nurture, and I felt very safe. There were 7 of us, and everyone played a certain role. This was my perception as a 5-year-old, the youngest child with My mom, and 6 other parents, my siblings. The Great joy of being the youngest, the baby of the family. It had great qualities.

This classy beautiful old fashion desert that brings wonderful memories and joy to my childhood. Follow my recipe and bake it and as it bakes, the smell your home as it fills with spices and joy (as if it was a smell)

I have put my own spin on this dessert, adding my own style based on the history of great cooking in my home.

YIELD
8-10 people

PREP TIME
40 minutes

COOK TIME
1 hour

INGREDIENTS
2 large loaves of Brioche or white bread, cut in cubes
1 cup of pecans or walnuts, chopped
2 oz of raisins
2 oz of chunk pineapple, chopped
2 oz of Maraschino cherries, chopped
1 cup of heavy cream
½ cup of milk
1 cup of butter
2 eggs, beaten
4 oz of brown sugar
2 oz of white sugar
¼ teaspoon of salt
1 teaspoon of cinnamon
½ teaspoon of nutmeg
1 teaspoon of pure Vanilla extract

GLAZE INGREDIENTS
1 cup of powdered sugar
2 – 3 oz of milk

DIRECTIONS
In a large bowl, combine milk, heavy cream, and beaten eggs. Stir and then fold in brown and white sugar, butter, salt, cinnamon, nutmeg, vanilla, and fruit with a plastic spatula. Add bread cubes. Fold in and place in the fridge for 15 minutes until the custard soaks into the bread. Preheat oven to 450 degrees Fahrenheit.

Grease a large baking dish with butter and pour bread mixture in. Put bread pudding mixture into the oven and bake for 1 hour or until golden brown. Place the baking sheet under in case any drippings. You will smell the sweet aroma throughout your home, indicating it's ready!

Optional:

Take powdered sugar and add 2 oz of water. Stir until smooth and drizzle over bread pudding for added sweetness. (I prefer it plain.) Enjoy.

FAMILY PHOTOS

ABOUT THE AUTHOR

Paulette "Paulie" C. Johnson Elliott is a licensed chef, who received her credentialing from Central Piedmont Community College, Culinary Arts Department in Charlotte, NC. She previously worked as an HIV counselor licensed by the New York State Department of Health and conducted HIV testing at Woodhull Health and Hospital Cooperation. Needing an escape, she found comfort in cooking.

In 2007, she diagnosed with a pituitary brain tumor and hyperthyroidism and failed adrenal glands. After retiring the following year, she then developed chronic asthma and sleep apnea. Although initially depressed, cooking brought back the joy she once had in her life. After receiving her qualifying food certificate, she began catering events, parties, business meetings, and family and church functions.

She is married to a wonderful man, Martin Elliott, who motivates and loves her and has one beautiful daughter named Janeece C. McDonald, and three stepchildren, Martin Elliott, Jr., Emanuel Elliott, and Janiya Elliott, who she loves dearly. Family is very important to her, and God is the center of her life. It is because of them that she was able to write this book and exercise her gift of cooking.

www.ingramcontent.com/pod-product-compliance
Lightning Source LLC
Chambersburg PA
CBHW041547220426
43665CB00002B/54